D0061557

Find Your Way Home

Words From the Street, Wisdom From the Heart

by the Women of Magdalene
with Becca Stevens

Abingdon Press / Nashville

FIND YOUR WAY HOME
WORDS FROM THE STREET, WISDOM FROM THE HEART

This book is printed on acid-free paper.

Library of Congress Cataloging-in-Publication Data

Stevens, Becca, 1963–
   Find Your Way Home: Words From the Street, Wisdom From the Heart / Becca
Stevens.
    p. cm.
   ISBN-13: 978-0-687-64705-7 (pbk. : alk. paper)
   1. Meditations.   2. Stevens, Becca, 1963–   .   I. Title.
   BV4832.3.S74 2005
   242—dc22

                                2005015053

08 09 10 11 12 13 14 15 16 17—10 9 8 7 6 5 4 3 2 1
MANUFACTURED IN THE UNITED STATES OF AMERICA

Contents

Acknowledgments

This has truly been a communal effort, with over a hundred contributors. One day Sigourney was asking the women to write, volunteers like Carolyn and Catherine were bringing food, twenty women were writing all morning, and interns like Ali were typing the writings into a document that we could edit later. Some of the early editors included Lindsay Kee, Richard Lodge, and Carole Hagan. Later editors included Sigourney, Gene, Stephanie, Jason, Carole, Marlei, and Cary. Baptist Healing Trust provided funding to help us create the book. Contributors include Regina, Sheila, Katrina, Marcus, Stephanie, Melissa, Gwen, Shaun, Lisa, Cindy, Jackie, Val, Tracey, Cynthia, Bev, Rosana, Nicole, Angela, Gladys, Meg, Kathleen, Kristin, Cheryl, Peggy, Nikki, and many, many more people and volunteers. This book could not have happened without the leadership of Carlana Harwell, the president of Magdalene's Board, and Toni Rodgers, the treasurer. Thank you to Gilbert, Cary, Joann, Dorinda, Tori, Rick, Rod, Pat, Dick, Connally, Sandy, Kay, Charlie, Cary, Jodi, and Peggy. We are grateful to the entire staff of Magdalene, including the directors of the program, Holli Anglin, Donna Grayer, Marlei Olson, and Cary Rayson. Their dedication and love make the program work.

Thank you to photographer Kristina Krug, all the thistle farmers, and all the volunteers, who make this journey so much more beautiful.

This book is dedicated to the women whom we have known who didn't find their way home, especially Julia, Peggy Sue, and the two Jane Does buried in Nashville, Tennessee. Thank God that love always has the last word.

INTRODUCTION AND INVITATION
BY BECCA STEVENS

In the sixth century, St. Benedict of Nursia designed the Rule of Benedict that for more than a thousand years has served as a model for communal living. Rooted in fidelity, hospitality, reverence, and love for all humanity, the Benedictine Rule calls for a balanced way of life in which "the heart becomes broadened with the unutterable sweetness of love."

Eleven years ago, another community was formed. Known as Magdalene, it is a community of women who have survived lives of violence, prostitution, and drug abuse. The women live together in houses for two years, free of charge, with no resident staff. After two years in the

Magdalene community, the women graduate, not to leave, but to become sisters who are committed to one another for life.

Out of their experience together, the Magdalene sisters, like the Benedictine brothers before them, have developed guidelines for living. Our rule is a simple guide for living in community. Consisting of twenty-four principles, along with some of the words and stories behind them, it describes practical ways we can love one another without prejudice or judgment. It is not meant as a rule in the conventional sense of restraining but rather of liberating. Taken as a whole, the rule can be thought of as a set of spiritual practices from which all of us can benefit.

In the Magdalene community, we start every day by gathering in a circle where we read a meditation, pray, and make sure everyone is all right. We share stories and wisdom. We tell the truth. In this book, we invite you to practice the spiritual principles of Magdalene. The book has taken a decade to write and has over a hundred contributing and anonymous authors. It includes the voices of women from the streets, dedicated staff, willing volunteers, and committed interns. Our purpose in writing it is to share our truth that in community, love and grace are the most powerful forces of individual and social change.

We have come to our truth through Magdalene, but we believe that all of us can benefit from these teachings and reminders of the way love works. In the setting of Magdalene, the teachings feel clear and direct. They are

stories of hope reminding us all that in whatever brokenness we know, the seeds of healing are sown. Our hope is
that the seeds of Magdalene will grow in the lives of read-
ers and in other communities around the country as our
words take root and multiply like thistles on the side of the
road in early spring.

While our story is particular, the problems of prostitution, violence, and drugs are universal. We have residents
from all over the United States and Latin America and
have met with women from widely scattered regions of the
world, including Russia, Ecuador, Botswana, Rwanda,
Sudan, and Thailand, all of whom tell similar stories about
how sexual abuse, not prostitution, is the oldest form of
abuse. That sad fact will never change until all agree that
it is never right to buy and sell women, that a community
cannot keep the secrets of a child abuser, and that the
exchange of money never makes it acceptable to abuse
another person for one's own benefit. We have never had
a resident come to Magdalene who has not been raped or
who has not known destitution.

Our work is a lifetime commitment, and it will be just
another drop of love in the grand scheme. Our goal is to
help one another move from destructive relationships that
tear up our bodies and spirits to healing relationships that
build them up. If you are reading these words from the
bunk in a prison cell, take comfort in knowing that part of
this book may have been written by a woman who sat in
that same prison. If you are reading these words in kinder

circumstances but know a bit about your own brokenness, we welcome you into our circle.

Besides introducing a way of living, this book is also an invitation to learn more about the community of Magdalene. After eleven years, we are thankful to know that in the midst of overwhelming problems, there is joy. For me personally, that joy is a source of strength. It gives me words to preach and prayers to offer. It provides a place to be healed, a well of forgiveness, and a feast of love. I cherish being part of a community where all of us are helping one another and all of us are givers and receivers.

The great lesson in this work has been that love can heal. I have been healed by listening, crying, and watching the women's courageous efforts. I have been healed by the wonderful witness of volunteers and staff who have given their hearts to this community. Through it all, I have learned that healing is possible for everyone, because our pasts are sacred ground in which love can grow new seeds.

Magdalene has taught me to try fearlessly, because the only thing we need to fear is not being able to love at all. This book is an open letter written to friends and strangers, inviting them to keep love alive and to offer it to others. I pray that in doing so, we will all find our way home.

In peace,

The Reverend Becca Stevens
Founding Director

Home is a woman I know well.
Her presence comforts me.
Her windows, like eyes, allow me to
    look out without fear.
I am safe with her.
Her clothes carry the scent of homemade
    soap and fruit from the orchard.
A soft, delicate, melodic voice.
I am here. I am here. Just call my name.
    I am here.
She reaches out to help all.
Takes thistles and turns them into flowers.
Browns. Reds. Greens. Different shades
    of orange.
She has special treasures just for me.
I love her for being here just for me.
The smell of cornbread she cooked.
The smell of flowers welcoming you.
Wearing comfort like a tiger wears stripes.
She was conceived in love and peace.
She will live long and teach many.

1.
COME TOGETHER

No matter where we are, we are better coming together than living separately.

We come on circuitous paths from prisons, from the streets, from churches because we are tired and want to live in hope.

We come in every color. We come lonely and afraid and do not want to die.

We come because our bodies and spirits are sick and our teeth are falling out and we know we need help.

I remember my last days using on the streets. I walked up and down Dickerson Road until a car stopped for me. I got in the car, and the man asked me to have sex with him. I agreed because I wanted that next hit of dope so bad. After we finished, he dropped me off at the store on the corner of Dickerson Road and Hancock Avenue. I saw the guy who I always bought my drugs from, and I bought dope. I went behind the store to take a hit. I smoked it on a glass stem and tried to forget what I had just done.

❧

When I came into Magdalene they gave me a key to the house. I kissed the floor because I knew that someone believed in me. I felt love for the first time in my life and wondered what kind of people were in this place. It made me tingle all over, from the top of my head to the bottom of my feet.

2.

PROCLAIM ORIGINAL GRACE

We are made in the image of God. We look at each person's journey beginning not with original sin but original grace.

Our journeys all start and end with God, and everything we do is a step toward our return to wholeness. Because grace is our beginning, we are worthy of all good things.

We are God's children in flesh and spirit. We never have to live in shame for all the things that have been done to us or that we have done to others.

It is hard for me to believe that I am made in the image of God. Lately, though, when I look in the mirror I can see God's child. I can look deep into her eyes and see that under the pain is courage, love, acceptance, willingness, open-mindedness, joy, self-worth, honesty, peace, truth, faith, humility, and my true self. What I want to say to my sister on the streets is that a time will come when you don't want to go on, but going on is a wonderful path that you can't even imagine. Today I say hold on to one thing and that is self. You were made in God's image.

❦

I come from a gated community in the south of Nashville. I had been taught my whole life that I needed to be safe, so I made that my primary concern. My family and I lived in a safe neighborhood, went to a safe church, attended a safe school, and never went near the unsafe parts of the city. It began to feel stifling and isolating to me. I decided to volunteer at Magdalene and began to sit in the circle with women off the streets. I found grace in that circle such as I had not known before. There was no judgment, just the realization that we are brothers and sisters walking as best we can toward God.

I have a broken body. I knew sobriety for nine years in
Magdalene and still am searching for peace. I have jumped off
hotel roofs to avoid the police and have survived being stabbed.
My body wants to be medicated to forget the brokenness and
all the times I abused it to get a fix. On my best days I know
even this broken mess of a body is a temple of spirit. I am trying to hold onto the knowledge that I began with God and I am
God's child.

3.
CRY WITH YOUR CREATOR

Even though we may feel lonely when we cry, we are never truly alone. Our despair is part of a larger chorus howling for justice that stretches back to the prophets.

We are working on our own recovery, and no one can do that work for us. We can listen to one another's stories and offer support as we walk this sacred ground.

Every step of the way we remind one another that God hears our cry.

*I was homeless, standing in the rain with nowhere to go
but into a car with a trick. I was sickly skinny, and my hair
was falling out. I was filthy, I had lost my front teeth, and my
clothes were dirty. I hadn't seen my family in twelve years.
I will never forget just standing at the edge of Dickerson Road
with tears running down my face. Someone help me.*

*I remember the first time I cried when I came into the
community two years ago. I felt touched by God, and it was
beautiful. I was lying in my bed on one of the very first nights
in the safety of this new home. I was looking around; and even
though I didn't see anyone there, there was a feeling of something inside of me. I can't describe it except that it was a feeling of love for myself. Because of this community of sisters and
God's mercy, I can face the big fears of my life.*

I think my old self felt there was so much pain with not much to gain. I felt the harsh words of others that held no grace. It left me feeling like there was no place to feel the peace of God. Now I can be loved and love without judgment. I can stay still and feel tears come and the words thank you coming from my heart.

4.

FIND YOUR PLACE IN THE CIRCLE

We are a disciplined community that consists of residents, affiliates, graduates, and women on the streets; staff, volunteers, board members, and community partners.

We find our place in the circle, knowing that it doesn't matter if on that particular day we will be giving or receiving.

Guests and newcomers are given priority in the circle.

I find this circle is like church for me—at least how church is supposed to feel. It feels like a loving group that is sharing a common goal, and there is no reason to try and take power or give up your voice. I am grateful for the image of the circle and amazed by the reality of it.

I sat in our circle and didn't feel anything. Then the director got up and walked over to a woman sitting near me and started braiding her hair. That is when I felt something growing in me, and I wanted to sing. Of course, the feeling was love. I had never sat in such a circle; and I was amazed as I watched her go to the next woman's hair, judging no one and being one of us. It was a comfort to have all the people in the circle be part of it. The circle was soothing and intimate, and it is changing my heart.

One morning at dawn I was walking the streets of Miami, and everything was silent. The only noise came from the creaking of a swinging gate. I had heard people talk about the gates of hell, and I wondered for a moment if I had died in the night and this was really hell. Coming into this circle is like being able to breathe again. In the circle it feels like I have come up out of the water and am tasting life. It is bright and blue. I can see more clearly. I can open my mouth. I can hear the birds and hear the waves.

5.
THINK OF THE STRANGER AS GOD

Instead of saying, "There but for the grace of God go I," we say, "There goes God." It reminds us of the truth that in loving our neighbors we are meeting God.

The heart of the matter is that God is in every person and that every person should be treated accordingly, with love and respect.

I couldn't speak English very well, and the judge was
telling me that I had to leave my child and go into Magdalene.
I was angry and couldn't believe that a man who did not even
know me was making me do this thing. What I didn't know
was that this stranger in the form of a robed judge was bringing
me a miracle. What that judge did makes it easier for me to
think of the stranger as God.

I used to get high under the walking bridge near downtown. I would get high and pray and listen to the birds. I really think the birds kept me going. One day I was sitting there, crazy as hell. I hadn't had a bath, hadn't eaten. I had a knife and was contemplating suicide when a man named Roy came and sat down beside me. He asked what I was doing. I told him I was tired and ready to give up. He invited me to go with him to a place called Mt. Nebo Church. So I went. When I got there they gave me clothes, let me take a bath, and fed me. Right after church several people were going to do an outreach on the streets. They invited me to come along. The women from the church were giving bags of toiletries and snacks away to women walking the streets. I saw them treat the stranger, me, with love. They were partnering with a community called Magdalene, and they invited me to come and live. The problem was I couldn't stay clean. It would take me almost another year to give up the drugs, but I am so thankful God didn't give up on me.

6.
TAKE THE LONGER PATH

There is no shortcut on the spiritual path. The journey to wholeness is lifelong.

We walk the path slowly and remind one another that love is waiting for us when we are able to receive it.

The journey is slow and miraculous; and our job is just to keep going, respecting love's power.

A power greater than myself finally brought me to sanity, and it was a special moment because I felt touched by God. I felt it when I entered into the Magdalene community. It didn't last long, but it was long enough for me to know that I was accepted as one of the sisters. It was long enough to see that I didn't have to live with violence, drugs, or abuse. That moment was just the beginning. Then the long time for healing started to set in. I am now in a process that just takes time. It takes time for growth. Now I am living in the time of waiting and watching myself and others grow spiritually.

❦

Recently at church, I saw one of the very first women of Magdalene walk into the service. This woman had made an impression on me because of her outgoing personality and her songwriting and performing. She had experienced a public reconciliation with her family, and it had had a profound impact on me. She had been on the streets for twenty years. People had thought she would never make it. She had fallen off the wagon a couple of times and gone back on the streets in dramatic fashion. I remember seeing her walking the streets on one of our outreaches after she relapsed.

As I watched her walk into church, I could see she was still fighting back. I couldn't help but think about what a long hard road this is.

7.

MAKE A SMALL CHANGE
AND SEE THE BIG DIFFERENCE

Sometimes the miracle of healing happens so slowly that we fail to notice the great difference in our lives.

Most of the changes in our lives occur in subtle ways. These subtle changes can lead to a difference that is big and profound.

The difference can set us free so we never have to buy or sell pieces of ourselves again to find meaning.

The change for me was to love my thoughts and even my memories. I remember the day I went to church and my grandmother sent me with her blessing, saying, "You must praise the Lord." I am loving that memory. I am praising the little pink dress and white shoes I wore that Sunday. I am praising how big the church doors were and how small I was. That memory may not seem important, but it is enough to change me.

The difference for me was having a home. I had just come out of jail, where I had to bunk with fifty other women. When I walked in, they handed me a key; and I could see a kitchen with pots and pans and plates. I almost dropped to the ground I was so thankful to have that key. I didn't want to lose it. It was small, but it kept me going for a long time until the lessons started taking root in me.

I stopped apologizing for what I believed. Then I stopped worrying if people thought I was a heretic or disrespectful. Then I started feeling like I could be myself and had more energy to love others. Then I felt excited about the ideas that were forming in my head, and I felt more confident that I could live out my faith honestly in my life. That is a huge change.

8.
LET GOD SORT IT OUT

In community our job is not to judge or say, "I told you so." We trust that God will sort things out, so we don't have to second-guess every decision someone else makes.

We are here to love one another in the most radical way possible, without judgment, and to pray that others can love us in the same way.

We give drink to the thirsty, food to the hungry, comfort to the sorrowful, clothing to the naked, and companionship to the imprisoned and dying. We wash one another's feet.

I was alone and scared, looking for a way out. I would get a hit to help the pain, and then I would run again and look for another hit. I would go into the mall and steal clothes to get more money. I even saw my son catch a murder charge on the TV. Now I have taken another chance. I am living in Magdalene.

It is only by God's grace that I am here at Magdalene. I can remember my last day on the streets. I was feeling so beat and troubled and heavy-hearted, and I got down on my knees and prayed that God would lead me away from crack and selling my body for crack. Well, about one hour later I was arrested for the last time and put in jail. This was God doing for me what I could not do for myself. Thank God for this. I now have five months clean, and I have found courage to keep going. It is a miracle.

It is not a problem to be lost. It is only a problem if you think it is impossible to find your way home.

9.

STAND ON NEW GROUND
AND BELIEVE YOU ARE NOT LOST

What we are feeling and experiencing is not a sense of being lost but the wonder of discovering something new.

This is sacred ground. We walk it alone, following the advice of others who have walked before us.

The prayer is to walk this ground in faith and trust that the Spirit leads us toward God.

My past is a land of unwanted, unloved, hard-knock living. My past tastes like a rotten apple that I have to eat because that is all there is, but in this community I am standing on new ground with God. I am standing on new ground that will withstand the earthquakes that I may cause. I am standing on new ground that is humble and filled with hope. I am standing on new ground that is waiting for me to plant my seeds and to spread seedlings around so others can blossom, too. I am standing on new ground because today I choose to walk a different direction. I am not lost. I have found my path.

The old familiar ground was to argue with people I love. I hate fighting, and I hate being so mad; but it takes a long time to learn how to treat people you love differently. It takes a while to find out that what lies below the anger is fear. I really don't think I raise my voice much anymore, but I still have to stop and check myself before I say something that can hurt someone just because I am feeling hurt.

Stepping onto new ground required courage and hope and a belief that things could get better. I didn't feel lost as I took those brave steps. There was companionship and love, though I couldn't immediately accept them. God gently took me by the hand as I made my way. I stood on new ground and yet felt that I had found my way home.

10.

FORGIVE AND FEEL FREEDOM

The scales of justice weigh more heavily on the poor and those who struggle in systems. It has never been fair, and the only way out is to forgive it all.

We are called to forgive all those who have harmed us. We are called to forgive all the harm we have done to ourselves. We are called to forgive all the people we have harmed.

Forgiveness allows us to move forward in peace.

I am from chaos and confusion. I am from my father's lap, crawling down after he's passed out. I am from a pony bottle of Miller Genuine Draft. I am from a closet where I hid from my father. I am from a bathroom watching the blood from the needle shoot to the ceiling. I am from a highway to hell on an early Saturday morning. I am from many schools. I am from dark alleys and early days. I am from my kids crawling out of my lap after I nodded out. I am from the smell of alcohol on many men. I am from addiction. I am from scorched Hamburger Helper that my babies had to eat. I am from March 13th, 2006. I am from a life of one to a life of many. I am from total darkness to pure light. I am from dying to recovering. I am from anger to forgiveness. I am from being nothing to being everything. I am from an addict in bondage to a recovering addict that's free.

Even though God has forgiven me, I sometimes don't forgive myself for my actions; but it's the only way I am free to be a better mother, sister, and daughter to my family. God has given me the opportunity to be free and to live a productive life today and to recover.

Sometimes I ask, "Why can't I forgive myself for the hurt and the pain I've caused?" Then I hear my grandmother's whisper in my ear: "Sissie, I have always been so proud to have you to love."

I have forgiven the man who abused me when I was a child. I can pray for him and hope for wholeness. That didn't come until after crossing a desert of hurt and then fording a river of confusion and confrontation and finally climbing the hill of acceptance; but I am so grateful that I know the sweet taste of forgiveness. I love that I can see that even in that pain there were gifts that I have used in my life. I marvel that part of who I am was born from that experience, and it makes me love the world more.

11.
UNITE YOUR SEXUALITY
AND SPIRITUALITY

We have been taught that our sexuality is a commodity and have learned to live in a spirit of mistrust and manipulation.

In community we claim ourselves again, saying no to people and institutions that are not part of the healing of our bodies, minds, and spirits.

We are sexual beings made in the image of God. We are spiritual beings made of flesh and bone. We are allowing one another the dignity of experiencing our spirituality and our sexuality.

I knew where I had been, but I just kept denying it all. I just kept everything a secret. It made me lose my voice and made me feel like I had no purpose. God. Oh God, of all the wrongs I've done, why? Why would you love me enough to let me live?

It was news to me that my spiritual life and sexual life were connected in my body. I remember waking up in a car that I had stolen and not feeling my body at all. Fortunately it was the police who woke me up, and that became the beginning of trying to feel my body and my life again. It has not been easy, and there have been great highs and lows. I know the sweetness of grief and the feeling of tears against my skin. I also know that I will still sacrifice just about anything to be accepted by a man. But knowing that my body and spirit are connected at least gives me permission to treat my body and every other body in the world as a great gift from God.

One of the first times I went to an event at Magdalene, I was surprised that the women were so dressed up. In my mind I thought that if they were looking so beautiful, they still must be acting out. Pretty quickly, though, I could see that it was my own misconceptions bleeding through. The women were showing outward and visible signs of a healthy union of sexuality and spirituality.

12.

SHOW HOSPITALITY TO ALL

We are called to offer hospitality to every guest, resident, staff member, stranger, and old friend.

We remember all the kindness that people have offered to us.

We treat everyone as a blessing and offer them something such as tea, handmade products, or a story to take on the road.

We go back to the streets and offer our gifts to the women who are still walking.

Hospitality is something I try to show by giving a kind word, showing concern, offering a shoulder to cry on, or cooking comfort food. I am trying to give back what has been given so freely to me. This is what hospitality is to me. I want to try and give unconditional love to someone who doesn't know what love is. It would be great to be there for a stranger who isn't that different from me.

I have been the recipient of hospitality. I was given a basket of personal products as soon as I came into Magdalene. I was offered dinner and clothes from my housemates and sisters. This was how I learned the concepts of how to show hospitality to others. Now I am on the giving end. When a new woman comes into our community, I find myself sharing with them. I want everyone to feel the blessings and unconditional love of community.

Before I came to Magdalene, I used to walk around the neighborhood where one of the communities was located. I was scared to go near the house and so were the other women and drug dealers. Then one day someone from Magdalene offered me a soda and a bag of chips and told me if I ever got tired there was a place for me. About a week later she gave me more food and kept offering me a place to come and rest. It was the greatest example of hospitality that I have ever witnessed. It finally took root, and one day I crossed the street and made my way up the steps and knocked on the door. When I left two years later with a full-time job, a car, and an apartment, I thought about how it had all started with someone offering me a bag of chips.

13.
LAUGH AT YOURSELF

The only way to survive communal living and have it be a spiritual experience is to allow humor to be part of it.

Finding the humor in anything is a sign of grace. We do not have to take ourselves too seriously.

If we can laugh at the small things that make us mad, they will not undermine our work or our community.

When I sat in the circle today and saw my new friend, a smile came to my face. Warmth filled my heart, and excitement fluttered in my stomach as I watched her. It would only take us looking at each other right now for the giggles to start and all concentration to be broken. She has no idea the laughter she brings to my heart—not just sometimes but all the time.

One of my housemates was cleaning the bathroom, and it was pretty clear from the way she was just spraying stuff in the tub that she wasn't taught about cleaning the way I was. Watching her drove me crazy and frustrated me. One day she came out into the living room after about five minutes in the bathroom and said she was finished cleaning. I was all over her and told her that I thought she was lazy and dirty. She came back with a list of things I was doing wrong. After a few minutes, we realized we were both right and that we all take shortcuts and hate to get caught. We starting laughing, and it saved the day. That was eight years ago. We are good friends, and we still laugh about that day.

There was a horrible tornado in Nashville in 1998 that
came right through the Magdalene house where I was living.
We were panicked and scared, and we hid in the closet. The
wind tore through the alley behind the house and broke out
some windows. When it was over, we stepped out of the closet
and looked around. Something was strange, but we couldn't
figure out what. It took us about twenty minutes; and then
finally one of the women said, "The gazebo! The gazebo is
gone!" That was it. There had been a beautiful wooden gazebo
behind the house, and it had disappeared in the tornado. It
struck us as a relief to figure it out and ridiculous that we had
forgotten what had been a huge landmark just thirty minutes
before. We laughed and laughed, and it made us feel better.

14.

CONSIDER THE THISTLE

The thistle blooms in streets and alleys where women walk and sleep.

We spend a lot of time considering the thistle— its rough exterior, its soft and regal center, and its capacity to break through concrete to blossom.

In a world that names them weeds, we taste the riches of thistles and savor their beauty.

We are thistle farmers. The world is our farm, and we harvest where other people do not want to travel.

I know Dickerson Road all too well. I lived there in abandoned houses, sheds, and lots. The smell of urine was everywhere. I kept all my worldly belongings in garbage bags. I spent hours looking for restaurants where I could wash my body off. I spent days going to thrift stores looking for free clothing. All of this so I could hang out at the gas station to panhandle or catch a trick, whichever came first. I had no shoes, no good clothes, nowhere to sleep, no food to eat; and yet I am beautiful and worthy of every good thing.

❧

I saw fear on people's faces when they saw me coming. I had no faith, and my spirit was broken. The only thing I could do and not have to feel was drugs and the very cruel lifestyle of it. One thing about the thistle, though, is that it still has life. I bloomed again, and now I can enjoy life free from addiction.

❧

In some things there is unity. In other things there is diversity. In all things there is God's love. That's the way I look at it. There were no weeds in Eden. Even the thistle was loved by God. I can see life in a thistle and how God created life in me.

69

15.
LISTEN TO A NEW IDEA

We are open to other perspectives about new ways of acting or thinking.

If we think that no one else understands us, we may dismiss some good and fresh ideas.

We want our lives to be changed by this journey, so we need to be open to being changed.

I'm sick of my own suggestions and tired of my own thinking. So give me a new idea, and maybe something good will come. I would love to succeed instead of fail, so I need some suggestions. I'm looking for a change. I would take some advice, and maybe it could save my life.

I remember when I surrendered myself. It was the biggest turnaround of my life. I got up one morning in the community and took my wig off. I took it off because I needed to be myself. I was ready to stop hiding and ready to start growing. I was ready to work with others and make some changes and see the real me. I wanted to be the person who has dreams and goals and lives them out. I wanted others to see me. I decided that day that I was beautiful even with my scars and messed-up teeth. I knew that God had new plans for me and because of his belief in me that nothing could hurt me.

❦

Drugs taught me how to be who I am—mean as a Rottweiler or gentle as a lamb. I could be a thief in the night and then try to justify how it's all right. Drugs taught me how to love my brother and lie to his face. I could look you in the eye, and you would never know I was lying. I could take a kind man for all he's worth. That is what drugs taught me, so I am in need of some better teachers.

16.
LOSE GRACEFULLY

If you are wrong, act with grace and carry on with the work of healing. It is the easiest way to move forward in peace.

Say you are sorry for whatever wrong you have done, ask for forgiveness, and let it go. It is not yours to worry about anymore.

It was a cold day about five years ago. I was on drugs and couldn't stop and didn't want to stop. I had grown up with drugs, and this was the world I knew. Once in the middle of the night, I had a fight out in front of a crack house. I was shot in my lower back; and then I shot my boyfriend, who died later. I went to jail and stayed in for three days. I ended up bonding out with my dad's help, and he introduced me to a sister of Magdalene; and that is how I found my way into the community. The women of the circle were such an inspiration to me and taught me how to let go of my past, accept the mercy offered to me, and grieve everything I loved that I had lost.

There was a volunteer I clashed with because both of us had control issues. I tried my best to practice spiritual principles with her; but she would just get under my skin, and I would hold a resentment toward her even though she was trying to help. There were a couple of specific times when she just had to be in charge. If something didn't go right, I was left to do the explaining and take the responsibility. She was a great spiritual teacher for me. It is only because of her that I learned to let go of some of my own control problems. Because of her

I gained some humility and learned again what it means to have a servant's heart. We have a much better rhythm now, and I can tell you that in my heart I love her and am grateful to her.

17.
REMEMBER YOU HAVE BEEN IN THE DITCH

We do not share the same experiences, but we all have been in need sometime in our lives.

We stay grateful for when someone lifted us out of the ditch and offered us food, clothing, or shelter.

We offer these gifts in gratitude with no strings attached.

The ditch is the place where I was beat up and beat down, with busted lips and black eyes. The ditch was where I was raped and was crying and screaming and thinking no one could hear.

🦋

My sister was rescued from a ditch. Her bus crashed while crossing over a bridge in Cameroon, Africa. She was going there to help teach and ended up being pulled from death by a kind stranger who happened to be traveling behind the bus. I will never forget how quickly she went from being there as a helper to desperately needing the help of others. If I let myself have the luxury of contemplation, the image of my sister being pulled from the ditch leaves me forever grateful.

🦋

Who are you to tell me I have done wrong? I'm asking, who are you to say that you will pray for me and that help is just around the bend? Just who are you to say that you are sorry that stuff happens and that I should stop whining? The only way I can know you is if you tell me you have been in the ditch, too.

18.
WALK BEHIND

On the spiritual path we are not asked to walk side by side as friends. We are asked to walk behind our God.

We are called to learn what servanthood means and to follow our spiritual path.

We need to be servants of one another, everyone with different jobs.

Coming into Magdalene I found women who had been where I was and had made it out safely. It was good for me to have people to walk behind. Walking in front would have been tricky, and I would have gotten lost. Following made it easier to put one foot squarely in front of the other.

❧

To walk behind means that I need to follow. It means I can share new ideas, give hope, and open my heart. If I walk behind, it means that I can look ahead and see the faces of my sisters looking back at me. I can see them smiling and laughing with great joy. I can imagine that one day it will be my face that is looking back, giving hope to someone who is walking behind.

❧

I walk behind those who started the journey before me. As I walk behind, I know my place is just as important as theirs. As I walk behind, I realize we all are walking behind a power greater than ourselves.

19.
LIVE IN GRATITUDE

Everything is a gift, so we can offer and accept it all with gratitude.

We contribute in gratitude for all we have been given so that our gifts can be offered to others with no strings attached.

Gifts given over and over eventually come around so the circle of love is completed. Everyone is giving, and everyone is receiving.

I give thanks to God for giving me this beautiful angel I met in Magdalene. I give thanks to God because he puts angels all around me, angels of love that I see guarding me and taking me in their care so I never dash my head against a stone. I give thanks to God for all the days that I wake up with this new way of life. I give thanks to God for my life today and everything God has given to me. Thank you.

I know that people write gratitude lists. I can never keep up with lists, but I do remember once walking up a big mountain and deciding that with every step I would say the name of someone I was grateful to. I started with my children and then began to think back on my life. The mountain was huge, and so I was able to say the names of grade-school teachers and people I barely remembered from camp. It was wonderful; and by the time I reached the top, I was in heaven.

I am trying to be grateful for my past. I am trying to be grateful for the last day I was using and for that feeling of being lost. I am trying to be grateful for the memory of my feet hurting and the blisters and how I kept walking until I found a place to rest. That kind of gratitude makes it easy to be grateful for all the good that has come into my life. That kind of gratitude makes it easy to be grateful for the sun on my face and the singing of the birds and for waking up.

20.
LOVE WITHOUT JUDGMENT

We love the women still walking the streets, the people who have turned away from us, and the people we thought we could not love.

This is the kind of radical love that can change the world.

We believe that radical love is experienced in how we serve one another in the name of our higher power.

Here at the Magdalene program, I have been learning that
to judge others is the biggest error I can make as a human being.
I've been learning that I do not like it when people judge me,
because in reality no one knows how I am inside. It hurts my
feelings when people laugh or talk behind my back. I am a
human like anyone else. I am teachable, adorable, and loving.
I am a little girl from God.

When I came into this community, I couldn't comb my hair. Just to think about touching it hurt because of the knots, but they loved me anyway and gave me a beautiful bed and hugged me.

I have not been a perfect person in Magdalene. After a relapse, I was welcomed back into the Magdalene circle. I was not as forgiving to myself as others were to me. People accepted me without judgment, and it overwhelmed me. It was the first time in my life I felt unconditional love. All that is expected of me is to do what is right for me. Sisterhood is welcoming no matter what.

I have learned not to point a finger at someone, because there is always something that I don't know and some reflection of me in them. We are all equal in God's eyes, and we should treat everyone accordingly. People didn't judge me at Magdalene, and that is how I can go back to the women on the streets and love them without expecting anything in return.

21.
STAY ON POINT

When we get busy with many distractions, it is easy to ignore our weaknesses and lose our focus of trying to live a clean and healthy life.

We are connected to God and to our neighbors and ourselves when we are on point.

We know that we are our sisters' keepers and want to serve one another well.

I am from a place where love comes hard, where prostitutes lose their lives trying to roll on a trick, where shootings are normal and closed caskets are a must. I had to keep my wits about me and learn to be my own best friend. From there I came into a loving home, where so much time has passed that sometimes I take my freedom for granted; but if I don't keep my focus, I may slip back into where I came from. So I'll take it one day at a time and do the best I know how. I want to make the best of where I'm at here and now.

❦

If I use all the tools provided me by this program and my sisters, I can suit up against life's challenges and stay on point. We are supposed to use everyone's wisdom, experience, strength, and hope. God envelopes us with beautiful angels who cheer for us. My sisters keep me on point, and God keeps all of them on point! The easiest way to stay on point is to have a broad base.

22.
PRAY FOR COURAGE

We pray for the ability to hear God's voice and know God's will for our lives.

We pray for the courage to walk the path of faith that has been set before us.

It is good to listen to God's call. It is good to pray for God's vision. It is even better to pray for the courage to live it out for the rest of our lives.

I pray for courage, which is a profound word for me. It is deep, tall, wide, and long. My journey has taken a mountain of courage, and only courage could have brought me home. I think that courage is teaching me that home is where my heart lies and that my heart needs to lie with God.

I pray to the Lord, "God, please give me strength to tackle all that lies in my path each day." He answers back, "I've got you covered in my arms each day."

Sometimes it does feel like I can hear the voice of God come quickly like the wind and whisper a passing thought, and then ever so often I have the courage to take that passing thought and discern the truth in it. Then once in a while I have enough courage to speak about that truth to others and act upon it. When I have had that kind of courage, it has always brought surprising and abundant results. That must be how the Spirit works when we are brave enough to believe in God's Spirit at all.

23.
FIND YOUR WAY HOME

All our journeys begin and end with God.

We are finding our way on this path toward wholeness and love.

We are helping one another find our way home from places as close as five miles and as far away as twenty years.

I remember the first day I came home. There were four beautiful women walking out onto the porch to say hello. I looked at the gated yard and had the strange feeling that it seemed familiar. I realized that I had lost my way long ago, and coming into this place gave me an almost forgotten sense of peace. When I walked in, there were plants everywhere; and I was crying because of the nice furniture. I loved the soft bed that felt completely different than the prison mattress I had just left. When I went into the kitchen, I rejoiced at the pots and pans, because I remembered the glass jars and spoons I had left on the sidewalk. This was the home I'd almost forgotten about. Thank you, God, for leading me home.

❧

I have a life and a home. I can turn a key and come in the place I call home. I can listen!

I can laugh and I can cry! I can find myself along the way! I am not alone!

❧

Life's worldly possessions are things most people cherish: cars; homes; jewelry; and, yes, sometimes family. But there is another life. It's called eternal life. The song says, "I'm gonna trade my earthly home for a better one, one day." I cannot wait to go to heaven. I know that's the place I want to go.

24.
LEAVE THANKFULLY

We are grateful when we meet each other; and we want to be just as grateful when it is time to part ways, to move on, or make a change.

We walk away from each other when we need to, with thanksgiving, not bitterness or resentment.

When we need to part ways, there can be well wishes and prayers for God's blessing on the next part of the journey.

I will be leaving in three months. The idea of leaving frightens me. I have been given so much the past twenty-one months. It is this gratitude that I feel will help me leave happily. I realize leaving will not be the end of my relationship with Magdalene. I will be a sister for life. I will take all my tools and recovery with me. My gratitude will continue. I will start the next stage of my life with a thankful heart and continue on with my journey happily.

When my time was up at a Magdalene, I was sad and scared and didn't know where the journey was going to take me. I was grateful for the third and fourth chances I had been offered, but I was mad that they were asking me to head out on my own. I knew it was going to take so much work, and I didn't want to give up this sanctuary that I had come to love. I see other women coming in, and they do not know how to be thankful. They look like they think they are owed the stuff that has been given to them, but I know that they just haven't learned what gratitude is yet. It will come, I'm sure.

There was a woman who came into our community who did everything she was supposed to do. When she made the decision to leave, a lot of folks didn't agree and expressed it. She could have gotten angry, but she just showed grace and said thank you to everyone. She still comes by and comes over. She taught me so much about being thankful and graceful in leaving. Now most of the wounds are healed.

Prayers answered
Blessings accepted
Love given freely
Gifts unspoken
Joy for friends
Tears for joy
Now it's my turn
Show gratitude
Give thanks
Show blessings
For every day
Thereafter

About Magdalene

Magdalene is a two-year residential and support community for women coming out of correctional facilities or off the street who have survived lives of abuse, prostitution, and drug addiction. Begun in 1997 in Nashville, Tennessee, Magdalene offers women at no cost a safe, disciplined, and compassionate community in which to recover and rebuild their lives.

Magdalene was founded not just to help a subculture of women but to help change the culture itself. The organization stands in solidarity with women who are recovering from sexual abuse, violence, and life on the streets, and who have paid dearly for a culture that buys and sells women like commodities. Magdalene stands as a witness to the truth that in the end, love is more powerful than all the forces that drive women to the streets.

To support the Magdalene residents, Thistle Farms was launched in 2001. It is a nonprofit company that makes all-natural body-healing products. Thistle Farms is named for the only flower that grows along the streets and alleys where the women walk. Residents, affiliates, paid staff, and volunteers operate this business to develop entrepreneurial job skills, decrease social isolation, share our message of hope, and raise much-needed funds for the program.

The Beginning

The Reverend Becca Stevens, Episcopal chaplain at St. Augustine's Chapel on the Vanderbilt University campus, founded Magdalene in 1997. She found working with the women who walked the streets to be a great gift. Her goal was modest: to create a safe place for the women, a home where they could find love as well as space, and time to work seriously on recovery. It needed to be a place in a residential neighborhood, with a kitchen, bedrooms with sheets, a living room with a sofa and chairs for gathering together, and flowers outside the front door. For many of the women, this would be their first real home. The three most important aspects of the residential community were that the women would never pay to live there, they could stay two years, and no staff would live with them.

The Houses

Not far from the Vanderbilt campus is an area known as Sylvan Heights. At the beginning of the Magdalene ministry,

Becca and her family lived in this neighborhood. She learned that the Campus for Human Development, another local nonprofit, would share with Magdalene a donated house down the street. Becca explains, "I never wanted Magdalene to be a 'not in my backyard' ministry. I wanted to be near the women, to have them in my house, and to be able to walk to theirs." Many community volunteers, members of St. Augustine's Chapel, and Vanderbilt students worked on carpentry and painting and found items to furnish the house. Soon five women in recovery moved in, each with an average of one hundred arrests and ten years on the streets. Over time, the deed to the house was given to Magdalene.

The second house, on Arthur Street in north Nashville, also was donated to the program. The third house was on Hillside Drive, also in Nashville. It was to be furnished in a style the women deserved, in keeping with the program's theology of "loving one another lavishly." With this in mind, a "wedding shower" was planned for the house. Beautiful china and other bridal gifts were registered at local stores.

The Dream

For the next house, the Magdalene community dreamed of something greater—a place built from scratch that would house eight women. A lot was found on the corner of Lena and Booker Streets, just off Charlotte Avenue, and was given to Magdalene as an anonymous gift. A fundraising drive brought in just under nine hundred thousand dollars to build the house. The city had never issued a permit for a group home in a residential area; but Becca felt strongly that this kind of home needed to be in a residential area, and the permit was granted.

When board member Gilbert Smith first took Becca to see the property, they saw drug dealers on both corners of the street. Gilbert said, "I'm not sure you want to be in an area like this. You want the women to get away from this kind of thing." Becca answered, "This is exactly the kind of place we want to be. We want to change the neighborhood."

Bee Thompson, an architect with the firm Moody Nolan Architects, offered her services as a gift to Magdalene. She drew up plans and oversaw the project from beginning to end, coordinating the work of the all-female team that included two architects, a draftswoman, an electrical engineer, a structural engineer, a landscape architect, and an interior designer. All the women donated their services.

Describing the house, Bee says, "The plan for the house is contemporary, with a large gathering room where all of the women from Magdalene can meet daily. The bedrooms are small to encourage the women to spend more time in the gathering room. The house wraps around an enclosed Serenity Garden, patterned after the interior courtyards in convents."

Gilbert Smith helped to obtain a building permit and found a lawyer, Leslie Newman, who volunteered his time for legal matters. Bob Plummer with Romach Contractors was awarded the contract. Gilbert explained, "I was in charge of the shell, Kim Norman did the interior, Tara Armistead planned the landscaping and the planting for the garden, and Cary Rayson and Hunter Armistead ran the capital campaign. The volunteers and the women of Magdalene did some of the construction, giving them a feeling of ownership."

The Magdalene women keep the house immaculate, not only seeing the space as their home but as a sacred space. When the house was completed in 2004, one of the residents said, "This is exactly what I have prayed for." Becca realized that for two years she and the volunteers had thought this was their vision, but it was truly a mutual vision. The staff and volunteers were the hands, inspired by the prayers of the women in jail and the women on the street.

The Community

For the Magdalene women, life in the community moves through a series of phases. When the women first arrive, they are initiates, meaning they are just beginning to live under a spiritual rule and need help from their sisters. After six months, they can move into the postulant phase, in which they are seeking guidance but are trusted by the group to make some decisions. During their second year, the women work through the phases of novitiate and candidate as they progress in their leadership and insight into community life. After two years, they are eligible to graduate and become a Sister of Magdalene, bringing the message of hope and love to new women coming off the streets. Throughout these phases, the Magdalene women celebrate and honor monthly achievements, including birthdays, sobriety birthdays, educational goals, new jobs, and more.

Magdalene currently offers services to women along the different stages of recovery. Each resident is given two years of housing, as described above. Magdalene graduates who complete the residential piece can participate in community gatherings and receive assistance in finding permanent housing. Graduates may help provide services to others still on the streets.

The Work

From the beginning, the work of the community was shared by the Magdalene women, staff, and loyal volunteers. The Magdalene women and volunteers quickly established a strong bond, a desire to know one another in the giving and receiving as they worked together. In many ways the two groups were different, and yet in so many ways they were the same: wives, mothers, dreamers, and seekers of a better world. Becca has always said that the line between priest and prostitute is very thin, and for the two groups of women that line began to disappear. One volunteer remarked, "I have been involved with many nonprofits who help people in need, but never have I felt the kind of energy caused by a pulling and gathering of strength as volunteers and Magdalene women worked together in community."

Much of the work, of course, requires money. Magdalene has never received any federal or state funding. It is important for all the money to be received with no strings attached so the program can be offered to the women as a gift. In 1998, Magdalene was asked to administer the Prostitution Solicitation School in collaboration with the Metropolitan Police Department, the District Attorney's Office, and the Public Defender's Office. The school is an eight-hour education program for men who are arrested as first-time offenders for soliciting prostitutes. All the revenue goes to support Magdalene.

Christ Church Cathedral in Nashville donated their Easter offering in 1997. That same year Magdalene hosted its first fundraiser. The following year, Cary Rayson, the first board chair, began writing grant proposals. Cary continues to be an active volunteer.

As Magdalene grew, the yearly fundraiser became larger and more formal. Yet it retained a certain intimacy, as many of the women in recovery participated by providing testimony, reading poetry, or singing songs. The event has continued to expand each year, as more people learn of the powerful work being done at Magdalene. Each year there is a theme, such as "Seeds of Hope" and "Let My People Go." Over the years, Magdalene has raised seven million dollars to support its programs through fundraisers, private grants, sales of products, and the solicitation school.

The Future

The work of Magdalene continues. In 2002, Magdalene Arms was launched in order to reach out to women still suffering on the streets of Nashville. Headed by Regina Mullins, one of the first Magdalene graduates, Magdalene Arms provides safe housing for up to four women on an emergency basis. Magdalene graduates return to the streets to distribute food, provide information, and pass out emergency kits to the women still living there.

The Nashville community has recognized and honored the transformative power of Magdalene. For her work, Becca Stevens was named Nashvillian of the Year by *The Nashville Scene* in 2000; and the Nashville chapter of the YWCA inducted her into the Academy of Women of Achievement in 2001. In 2002, the Center for Nonprofit Management named board president Cary Rayson the Kraft CPA's Board Member of the Year award for her leadership. In 2005, the Bank of America honored Magdalene with a Local Hero award. That same year, Becca Stevens was given the DuBose Award for Service by the School of Theology at the University of the South.

Magdalene continues to thrive and benefit from your prayers. There are currently five houses and a safe house for outreach. The community has built and blessed houses for graduates. Thistle Farms is a blossoming cottage industry with twenty employees, dozens of volunteers, and five interns. Sites have been selected for future homes, and sister communities have been established in Chattanooga and Charleston. Each year Magdalene slowly and purposefully grows, learning from mistakes and continuing to trust that love will prevail.

The Message

The women of Magdalene believe that love is the most powerful force for change in the world, and we are the witnesses to that truth. It is a truth that is revealed in slow and miraculous ways through the practices described in this book.

Love is tender and deep. We learn more about love every day as we speak in homes and community groups across the country, reaffirming the knowledge that Magdalene is not just about helping a subculture of women. We all need one another to be well. At the center of the mystery of recovery is the power of love, and love makes us sing.

To Help

If this book inspires you to help, here are a few suggestions:

1. Visit *www.thistlefarms.org* for more information.
2. Take a picture of thistles growing in your city and send it to Thistle Farms to be used in our thistle gallery.
3. Suggest the book to a friend, colleague, or book club to help educate others about the myths and realities of women living on the streets.
4. Buy a copy of the book for a local library or prison.
5. Encourage your local bookstore to carry the book and become a retailer for Thistle Farm products.
6. Write a review of the book for an online bookstore or blog.
7. Give this book to a woman you meet on the streets, along with toiletry items and information about Magdalene or other programs closer to you that may help.

Magdalene receives the entire author's proceeds from the book.

With thanks and love from the women of Magdalene and Thistle Farms.

We sing because we're happy.
We sing because the fire is hot in our bellies.
We sing because the wind is cool on our faces.
We sing because God is wonderful.

We sing because God is faith.
We sing because faith is hope.
We sing because freedom is a gift.
We sing because it makes the world go 'round.

We sing because God likes my voice.
We sing because we're free from bondage.
We sing because our souls can't be quiet.
We sing because today is a reprieve.

We sing because our mothers' wombs gave us life.
We sing because our fathers' hands hold us with love.
We sing because we gave life to our children.
We sing because we gave life to ourselves.

We sing because the season is changing.
We sing because we can show love pure as snow.
We sing because we're surrounded by our sisters.
We sing because our sisters' voices awaken our own.